EMOTIONALLY UNSTABLE

How I realised I'm mentally ill and came to terms with it... Mostly

Chelsea Parker

Author: Chelsea Parker
Editor: Megan Unwin
Photography: James Parker

Dedicated to the memory of

Brenda Mavis Voce
1936-2017.

She struggled before mental illness was widely
acknowledged or tolerated

CONTENTS

Acknowledgements   i

Introduction   ii

1   Part One: Realisation   1

2   Part Two: Proper Mental   33

3   Part Three: Ranting and Raving   47

4   Part Four: Acceptance   61

5   Part Five: Tips and Tricks   73

Final Words   93

ACKNOWLEDGEMENTS

~

I would like to thank the people who make my life possible by offering unconditional love and support in times of need. Those people are:
My loving husband, Jim Parker;
My mother and kindest person I know, Tina Maycock;
My long suffering sister who grew to love me, Shanna Maycock;
My uncle and venting companion, Tim Voce;
My three closest friends, Ellen McGhee, Danielle Bannister and Richard Armes;
My unexpected kindred spirit (and fellow freak show) Megan Voce and;
All members of 'HHELP' group, Hucknall.

For assisting me in proof reading and encouraging me to publish, I would also like to thank: my editor, Megan Unwin; fellow writing enthusiast, Chris Davison and; long term friend and mental health champion, Mhairi Levison.

INTRODUCTION
Mental illness

~

I always knew I wasn't like other people
What I didn't know, was how to put that into words

~

Dear Reader,

I don't believe there are many people out there who choose a life of chaos. Who decide to be a mentally unstable, emotional mess. Unfortunately, this life is thrust upon us.

In my experience of the mentally ill, and there are a lot of us out there, we tend to fall into one of two categories. The extra lucky ones get to be both.

Category A people, were born with a genetic predisposition and inherited a chemically imbalanced brain. Through no fault of your own (or anyone else) you were dealt the over emotional card at birth. Part of your brain is over-sensitive and always opts to work overtime. It could be the miserable part (depression), the fight or flight mode (anxiety and anger disorders), or the compulsive section (OCD). For any fellow bipolar sufferers out there the following may sound familiar: what causes an average person to feel sad makes me distraught, what causes an average person to be happy sends me hypomanic, and events that would elicit a strong reaction from an average person... Well, the reaction there

ii

could be anything from heartbreakingly tragic to downright hilarious!

Category B people are suffering trauma. That could be anything from being abused to being involved in an accident. Your experience screwed up the way your brain is wired and has caused a whole range of difficult to cope with moods and symptoms. The phrase 'that scarred me for life' applies here, without exaggeration. The good news here is that something broken has a chance of being fixed! There may be a few dents or cracks which stay on show, but with time and gentle effort the right specialist can get anything working like new.

Here's hoping.

To complicate things in ways only the brain knows how, trauma can also trigger a dormant predisposition. Similarly, a genetic imbalance can cause you to take risks which lead to experiencing trauma. This gives you double trouble, or what I like to call: never-really-stood-a-chance syndrome.

I personally believe I inherited a chemical imbalance. Emotional and mental difficulties are common in my extended family, I share various symptoms and behaviours with a grandmother I never spent a great deal of time with, and I had my first emotional breakdown at the age of four. I also had the misfortune of losing my dad to cancer while I was a teen which likely added to my becoming a beautiful mess.

Of course, this is all theory based on my experiences and musings. You probably have your own understanding of mental illness which fits into your life and your own thoughts. Social scientists have been trying to figure this stuff out for decades and are still arguing over nature vs nurture, so I'm not expecting to nail it after a few years of semiconscious self-reflection. But I will suggest if you are reading this as part of a self-help regimen, it may be time to accept you never had a choice in the brain you received, the genetics you inherited or the trauma you experienced. It is not your fault. You are not alone. And, you are allowed to understand 'mental illness' in whatever way helps and makes sense to you.

In the early months of 2015 I discovered mindful writing. Essentially it's just writing without care: don't think, just write! I wrote mindfully before bed. It allowed me to dump all the dark clouds floating around my brain onto paper, making it easier to sleep.

At that time my notebooks read like the angry ramblings of a lunatic and were eventually binned or burned. But as time has gone on, my writing (perhaps journaling is a truer description) turned into story telling as I began to make sense of my thoughts and experiences. This book is a collection of thoughts, life experiences, much needed reflections, occasional suggestions, and even a poem or two. I consider it a short (yet erratic) autobiography with some soft self-help thrown in for good measure.

The chapters aren't chronological, but themed to show my reflective journey from initially suspecting I had a problem (*Realisation* and *Proper Mental*) to accepting myself as an over feeling individual who needs help to live and function (*Ranting and Raving* and *Acceptance*). Emotionally, they are stages of suspicion, denial, anger, and then acceptance. My reality involved repeatedly circling back from anger to suspicion before eventually accepting help. The final *Tips and Tricks* section shares tactics and habits I've found useful that could be helpful to others should they resonate with my story.

I have tried to be as open and honest as possible, hoping to give an insight into my experience of living with mental illness. If sharing this helps even one person feel less alone in their struggle or recognise mental illness wasn't a choice they made, then I will consider it worth writing.

Chelsea Parker
2020

PART ONE: REALISATION

~
The first step is admitting you have a problem
~

I suspect I spent a long time in denial about my mental health. Some of it may have been ignorance because the only person I know how to be is me. I've never experienced feelings as anyone else so I can't compare my experience of love, grief, or sadness, to the feelings of others. But I now recognise my reactions to feelings are different to most people and I am easily distressed by emotion.

As a teenager and young adult I occasionally considered the idea that I might have a mental illness. This was usually following a particularly dramatic episode or when odd behaviours were pointed out to me
"Why is that girl talking to herself?" would usually do the trick.

But then I'd be okay for a while and any concerns would go on the back burner. I'd tell myself I needed to stop attention seeking, getting upset in public, or losing my temper. I should get control of my emotions and hide them away, like everyone else seemed to.

I needed to just stop being such a freak and make sure no one had reason to refer me to a counsellor!

But this promise made to myself would last only until the next meltdown.

Luckily I'm quite book-smart, so despite many signs and symptoms I managed to attend school, college, university and work with minimal days absent. When my depressive symptoms were severe I scraped by doing the bare minimum, then when I was well (or hypomanic) I'd manage to catch up quickly and be a high functioning student or employee. But for all I knew, everyone worked that way. It wasn't until I had a severe depressive episode, which led to me being out of work and medicated indefinitely that I finally accepted my fate and started to work on strategies for wellness.

Ignoring it wasn't making it go away...

Alpaca Farm Anyone?

~

An alpaca is a Peruvian cattle.
Adorable. They look like a sheep had a baby with a giraffe!

The first time a doctor mentioned 'bipolar disorder' to me I begged her not to refer me to a psychiatrist with what I imagine was a look of both fear and desperation: I'm not crazy! I went straight to my mum's, a blubbering mess of tears and snot (a sight she is all too familiar with).

"Bipolar" I said, "Surely not?"
Depression, perhaps. I could accept feeling drained and tearful and being frightened of answering the office phone was not my usual style of working. Desperately waiting for the weekend so I could hide in my flat, sleep and cry wasn't quite the 'Friday feeling' my colleagues talked about either, and letting that homeless lad sleep in my flat may not have been the best strategy for self-harm prevention. But I don't have manic episodes!

Sure, I'm happy and hyperactive sometimes, but isn't everyone? I like to be loud and dance around occasionally, but people should just loosen up and enjoy life! Setting up that business was a bit of a mistake. As was spending all of my savings on a master's degree I never finished. But it's not as though I'm in debt!

That was when my mother gave me the spoonful of realisation I needed in what we now refer to as 'the alpaca incident':

"Remember when you were going to take a twenty five grand loan out to set up an alpaca farm?"

... No.

The initial answer is no. Then the memories flood in. In 2015 I saw some photos of alpacas (you know the memes - 'Fancy a picnic? Alpaca lunch!') and fell in love instantly. Nothing could be better than having a furry alpaca friend! I found several acres of land nearby, enquired about a quote, started planning alpaca treks, meditation with alpacas, a rescue centre. I found alpacas online in need of a home. Researched a loan I could take out based on my (then) salary.

Maybe this was my life's purpose!

Maybe I could live on the land with them!

Maybe there could be a tepee!

My alpaca dreams never materialised, thankfully. Loans and pets are a big commitment. Mum tried to talk me out of it and met the usual chorus of "Why are you trying to hold me back?"

Then I came down from my cloud, entered a depressive episode and 'the alpaca incident' stayed forgotten.

...I still receive alpaca themed gifts for birthdays and Christmas!

Still, I Keep Trying
Psychiatrists, psychologists and psychotherapists

~

Should it bother me each of these titles implies I'm a psycho?

There are levels of psycho-ness you discover on entering the mental health sector. Psychotherapists are fine; they help reshuffle your way of thinking if you're going through a difficult period or think you're losing the plot! I recommend all humans visit a therapist during stressful times (seriously, we all get stressed and it might help). Psychologists come into it when you need something specialist; your symptoms are specific or becoming complicated. When psychiatrists start getting involved, you know you have a problem.

I avoided any form of therapy until I was twenty three, on sick leave, and felt backed into a corner. I was opposed to therapy for two reasons: (1) why would I want to talk to a random stranger about my feelings? I can barely comprehend the emotions I go through, never mind putting them into words; (2) what if I talk to someone and they think I'm completely nuts? I wouldn't suit a strait jacket.

When I eventually began to engage in therapy I found it distressingly difficult, especially on occasions where the therapist or setting didn't work for me.

I noticed times when I had been failed by the system and

realised part of the difficulty was that I needed more help than is standard.

~

March 2015

After a six month wait on the NHS, Clare arranged to meet me in a library. I could hear her chatting through the door as I waited: not ideal. She was friendly in greeting me and gestured to a chair. The table and laptop between us made a physical barrier, as though I had arrived for an interview. Clare then locked the door, blocking my escape route and trapping me in the room.

"I haven't had time to read your notes" she said, "but I've made a quick call and found out you have depression and anxiety". After this sentence my professional alarms are already ringing.

I managed twenty minutes of question answering in the interrogation room of no escape and wondered how many questions could have been avoided had she read my notes. Once I couldn't take anymore, in between sobs and with the need to flee overpowering me, I stood up. So did Clare, positioning herself between me and the door.

 "Sit down" she said.

No.

I need to run, far away. Then curl up in the foetal position.

I stepped towards the door and Clare did the unthinkable: she pulled me into an embrace.

The door is so close...

But it's locked.

I need her to open it...
But she's hugging me.

SENSORY OVERLOAD:
~~Fight~~
~~Flight~~
Freeze
I'm glad I'm a natural pacifist.

Aftermath:
Clare wrote to my GP saying I needed cognitive behavioural therapy immediately or I would have a massive relapse.
I refused to access talking therapies for over a year.

~

April 2016

The turquoise therapist was more style than substance. I'm not suggesting she wasn't qualified, just that her approach consisted mostly of agreeing with everything you said while using a soft voice.
What Turquoise did well, was create a safe space; a comfortable lounge where you could chat, cry, or gaze out the first floor window without the worry of being seen. A setting I would recommend to anyone in need of a good rant, a destressing cry, or to talk something through to an unbiased ear.
Unfortunately, my brain is more complicated than that.

~

February 2017

Dr. Short was fantastic. I accessed her through an employee assistance scheme. My employer was paying but sessions took place out of work and there would be no feedback given to work.

Every workplace should subscribe to this!

Dr. Short put me at ease instantly. She had worked for *Childline* which was perfect at the time as I had been experiencing flashbacks from childhood and adolescence. She gave my 'inner child' a place to breathe and heal. Each time I left a session I felt better, more whole.

Unfortunately, I was off my meds and suffering a gradual decline. I forgot to eat for days, collapsed from exhaustion and couldn't get out of bed to go to work.

No work = No employee assistance scheme = No Dr. Short.

The Silver Linings:

I accepted I had an illness;

A talking therapy had actually helped;

I realised I had to find specific therapists who worked well with me!

~

January 2018

Round 1:

A full consultation with the Community Mental Health Team after a lengthy waiting list.

"Do you have any history of self harm?" The doctor asks.

"Cutting and smoking"

"Suicidal ideation?"
"Sometimes it's all I can think about"

"Experienced euphoria?"
"Occasionally I feel in touch with the universe, sense my life flow is connected to the planet, and think I'm here for a special purpose"

And it goes.
The conclusion is that I have bipolar disorder alongside borderline personality disorder, which may have caused some confusion and misdiagnoses.

March 2018

Round 2:
"I met with the team and the psychiatric consultant. We think you have traits of an emotionally unstable personality but don't want to give you a diagnosis... I'll write to your GP to let them know you've been discharged...
We recommend you try yoga..."

~

May 2006

A flashback to: The education system.
Let's call this exactly what it is: ticking a box.

I am unsubtly pulled out of a maths lesson in front of thirty students who assume if you are removed from a class it's because you're in trouble. Escorted to an unfamiliar part of the building, I sit in front of an unknown woman with an unfriendly face and no idea why I have been summoned.

"Hello Chelsea, would you like to talk about anything?"
"... No"
"Okay, you can go back to your lesson"

Box ticked.

~

Presently, I see a psychologist every three months. She came recommended and it's obvious why: her approach feels individualised and fits around what I need. She helped me create a management plan to minimise my symptoms and now sessions are an easy check-up. How am I? What's been working? What has life been throwing at me?
It's private and expensive, but worth every penny! And it only took twelve years and eight counsellors to find her.

When All That's Left is a Fake Smile

~

Sometimes smiling is the biggest farce. It's up there with the words 'I'm fine' when you need to feign normalcy. If you can laugh, joke and smile, no one will realise your heart is bleeding.
Hide behind the words.
Hide behind the grin.
You might even kid yourself.

But when the others have gone and you find yourself alone, once the smile has faded, that familiar darkness creeps in and opens up the wound in your soul.

Don't tell anyone though; you wouldn't want to upset anybody.

Don't be Fooled
Alcohol is never the answer

~

I was ripped from my sleep by a man telling me we had to leave. I couldn't remember his name and didn't know where I was. The fire alarm was annoying but I felt exhausted and the bed was so comfy! I was alone. Shame really, because I wanted a cuddle; wouldn't have minded who with.
My feet were cold. No socks! Those dolly socks were always falling off but they were my only pink ones and my favourite! I wasn't leaving without them.

~

I was ripped from my sleep by a man telling me we had to leave. I think his name was Daniel. Sitting up I noticed the faint aroma of vomit. An alarm was ringing. What floor were we on?

~

I stood outside the biggest multi-storey apartment block I had ever been in with no idea where I was. Was it 4am or 2? I really didn't care, I just wanted sleep. My memory was foggy but I had some idea it was us who had set off the alarm and sensed we were in trouble. I vaguely recalled Sean urinating in a sink and a fridge full of gone-off milk. We walked away from the evacuation point and headed uphill; the route unfamiliar.

Dragging one foot in front of the other took all my strength. Feeling weak, my heart pounded against my rib cage. Keep going. I couldn't say how much I had drunk, what I had drunk, or when I last ate.

It was James who had been sick. Paul lit a scented candle to cover the smell but placed it nicely on a paper napkin. Joe panicked, tried putting it out with a fire extinguisher but succeeded only in eating a face full of foam...
Then the alarm had sounded.

~

I woke in a dimly lit snooker hall, slouched on an old sofa. 6am approached; the trams would start running soon. Then I could go home and pass out until late afternoon.

Just another Tuesday!
I never did get those socks back...

Identity Crisis
I wonder who today will bring

~

I look different in my head than I do in the mirror. In my childhood dreams I was a young girl with thick curly locks, a far cry from my straight blonde hair. Even now I have accepted my face, I imagine it thinner, more symmetrical and am occasionally caught out by my reflection: "That's not me, is it?"

It's not only my face I can't make sense of. It's my gender, my sexuality, whether I belong to a subculture. Everything about my body, my identity and my personality feels wrong. Something deep down inside me is broken and I don't fit. I just can't pinpoint where the wrongness is or how to fix it.

~

Blonde, Brunette, Silver Grey, Auburn, Violet-Black, Red, Mahogany, Chestnut, Strawberry Blonde, Golden Caramel, Chocolate Brown, Platinum and I still can't find a colour that fits.

When I'm feeling the hippy vibe, you'll find me with vegan approved pink flamingo hair, matched with an elephant print light cotton tee shirt and harem pants, while I walk around barefoot with a braided anklet and a nose stud.

Dark feelings require black hair, dark jeans and a baggy

sweatshirt (probably featuring a band logo with the hood pulled up). Together with Dr Marten boots and black mascara on my white-blonde lashes.

Embracing my inner nerd involves thick rimmed glasses and rocking a lot of checked shirts.

Fresh characters feel good. Until they don't anymore. Then I try the next person on for size.

~

I have a very specific memory of realising I liked both boys and girls. I was ten, still in junior school. There were sexual feelings involved and I remember wondering if you could have a boyfriend and also a girlfriend. The memory and confusion is vivid and I still remember to which boy and girl I was referring. From this you could conclude that my initial sexual orientation on reaching puberty was bisexual. Or just, greedy.

Throughout my teenage years I was attracted to girls but wanted boys to fancy me. An odd triangle of emotion and probably a mixture of peer pressure, teen magazines and needing to conform at school (by being pretty and popular - I failed). I was fourteen when I first 'got off' with a boy. I was also fourteen when I first 'got off' with a girl ('getting off' is what kissing, snogging, or 'making out' was called at my school during the noughties).

By the age of sixteen I realised I wasn't a girl and longed to play football and be one of the lads. I cut my hair short then messed around with hair wax, styling gel and dye. My usual blonde was turned a gingery brown; an attempt to look like a different person. I took to wearing hoodies, tracksuits and sports bags. I sat slouched in what I thought was a 'masculine' posture and when strangers referred to me as male or other kids wondered aloud if I was a boy or a girl I complained, but secretly revelled in it. One friend referred to me as his 'wing woman' and we'd go out to 'pick up birds' with limited success.

When my hair grew out (and was subsequently attacked by every colour of hair dye I could get my hands on, in quick succession) I returned to my act of heterosexual female: dating boys whilst avoiding any sexual activity and considering penises to be purely tools of rape.

As an adult my sex drive is about as turbulent as everything else about me. There are times I can't get enough and times where any is too much. When in relationships with men I consider myself 'straight' and when with women I consider myself 'gay' -I've never gotten on with the word lesbian. A new line I keep hearing is that sexuality is fluid; if I say this you can loosely translate it to: I can't be bothered to get into this conversation and couldn't care less what category of human you want to put me into.

I still think I'd have made a better boy.

~

What do you want to be when you grow up?

Accountant is the sensible answer. I have a logical, mathematical brain and its lucrative employment. I can imagine myself working away in an office, wearing a fitted suit and looking busily important as queen of the nerds.

Then I flunked my A Level Accountancy module. Damn!

Health and Wellbeing practices keep me going and are becoming increasingly popular in this stressed out capitalist regime in which we are captive. Having my own business would be fabulous! I'm not greedy, just need to pay the bills. The first diploma is in *Teaching Meditation*, the second, *Relaxation Therapy*. I set up a comfortable meditation room and advertise locally by distributing leaflets. I have regular sessions with clients for one to one relaxation and drop in meditation classes.

Then I start a shift pattern and can't do anything on a regular, weekly basis. Damn!

Teaching! That's a real 'career' path. I have experience working in schools, I've taught the occasional A Level lesson, and I'm excellent at the paperwork side of things. I've already acted as a cover supervisor and a registration tutor. I'm at least as smart as half the teachers I know and my degree results are better than some of my teacher friends. I could even be more 'well rounded' than a few, having had other jobs and life experiences instead of going straight into teaching from university.

Application Unsuccessful. Damn!

A travel blog is the way forward! There are genuinely people out there who are paid (or sponsored) to travel to places and blog about it! If they can, why can't I? I've already got half of Europe under the belt that I can blog about retrospectively.

I know a tech guy who offers to develop a blogging platform for me and host it on his server, then I'm up and running. After a few short months I have a decent page count, visitor count, thousands of Twitter followers, friends who have

joined in with blogging giving a global scale of destinations, and a local travel company have contacted me to discuss potential free trips in return for positive feedback!
Then tech guy and I have a fall out and the site evaporates. Damn!

Lecturer and researcher sounds like a great future! I struggled through university mentally and emotionally but I enjoyed the academic side of things; books, studying, and essays. I would love interviewing subjects for a social science study or presenting a controversial topic to a room of eager eyed students. I am accepted onto a master's course and start working towards becoming Dr. Chelsea!
But a change in circumstances means I can no longer afford the term payments. Damn.

LLAMA WHISPERER!
Not an actual job? … Damn!

~

My entire life has involved people calling me Chelsea. I never had a say in it and I'm still not convinced that's my name. Something feels wrong and with my Hucknall (Nottingham) accent I can't even pronounce it well. I'll answer to it but it'll answer to almost anything. My most common misnaming's are Josie and Charlotte, but I'm also regularly Cheryl or Claire. I once made a friend who after several meet ups realised my name wasn't Emily. A lecturer insisted my name was Jessica and it took a neighbour three years to stop calling me Kerry.

In late 2016 something was wrong but I couldn't place it. I changed job, moved flat, adopted a vegan lifestyle, pierced my nose, cut my hair and dyed what was left of it red, but the wrongness wasn't fixed.

Maddison was my name of choice. Maddison Maycock had a nice ring to it (Maycock being my maiden name) although I thought a full name change might be better. Taking my mum's maiden name was tempting; Voce is uncommon with a lovely Italian feel to it. I thought it might give me a sense of belonging with my mum's family too, rather than my usual outsider feeling.

It costs just £36 to change your name by deed poll! You don't even need a reason, just send off the paperwork...

I never got around to this and I'm glad. It would have been just another thing to change every time I felt ill.
The answer to 'have you ever been known by any other name' could have gotten way out of hand. I already have to list eight addresses for the 'places you've lived in the past five years' question during the yearly CRB check.

It wouldn't have fixed the wrongness either.

Home Sweet Home

~

I land on German soil and relax.

Finally, I can breathe again; I'm exactly where I'm supposed to be.

I catch a tram towards the centre of Bremen, passing familiar houses and listening to the familiar language of Deutschland: home at last.

The feeling of relief fills my heart and my eyes well up as I am overwhelmed by nostalgic emotion...

I am not bilingual, I am not of German descent and I had never been to Bremen before.

No Matter Where You Run, You're Still the Same Person When You Get There
Postcards from Chelsea

~

I've been to 27 countries in 27 years. It's a shame I don't remember more of it. My partner is both amused and annoyed by my inability to remember places I have been.
"It's lovely here!" I say.
"That's what you said last time we visited" he replies.

I am also asked "what is X country/city like?" from time to time and have to respond with an "I don't remember".
Of course, when I receive the question electronically, by text or through social media, I have the option of asking Google to recommend activities or landmarks and avoid any awkwardness.

Apparently I visited Gozo, Malta in 2008 and Wroclaw, Poland in 2012. An *Interrail* ticket proves a visit to Stockholm, Sweden in 2014, and I have a lovely photo of myself at the Trevi Fountain in Rome, Italy from 2011. Sometimes a photograph or discussion will trigger a memory and I can add a new, yet old, experience to my collection. But unfortunately, whether it's due to my medication intake or too many overwhelming emotions forcing me into autopilot, I may have some travelling ahead of me to re-remember places I have forgotten.

It may also be down to the stress and excitement of travelling but I've found I experience heightened emotions when visiting new places and travelling abroad. Obviously, this has resulted in memory loss, or suppression, on occasion. But, it has also meant I've had some of my most joyous, enlightening and terrifying moments whilst roaming a foreign land.

~

Dundee, Scotland, 2010

I can't sleep. In fact, I've not slept since my arrival three days ago. The bedroom feels wrong and I've experienced deep waves of unease since I got to this place. I take a shot of liqueur then nip outside for a quiet cigarette, not wanting to disturb anyone at 2am.
Re-entering the room my decision has been made. I throw my few belongings into a bag and head out. After a thirty minute uphill hike which couldn't go fast enough I reach a dark, closed station. The departures board shows that no direct trains go close to home. The anxiety slowly turns to resignation as tears fall down my cheeks. I sit with my pathetic luggage and try calming myself with another cigarette before facing the walk back. At least it's downhill this time.

~

Whitby, England, 2010

The cottage is perfect for our group. It's out of the way, big enough for ten and close enough to visit seaside towns. I get to share a room with my wonderful best friend, whose birthday we're celebrating. The feeling of wrongness is with me but I try to ignore it and join in the activities.

After a few evening drinks, plans to go into the nearby town are drawn and panic sets in. I can't go. I hide in the bedroom and cry silently on the floor, holding my knees to my chest. When I've managed to calm myself and have checked that my eyes aren't betraying me, I let Ellen know that I'll be staying at the cottage while they get dressed up and head out. Once alone, I check every window and door is secure before curling up on the sofa where I am free to cry in peace.

The feeling of being watched haunts me all evening but I control my breathing (mostly) and distract myself with *The Graham Norton Show*. When I run out of tears I crawl into a cold bed and try not to have a panic attack before the gang return.

~

Pisa, Italy, 2011

I scream at someone in a hostel stairwell until she eventually cries and a friend comes to comfort her. To this day I don't know what happened, who they were or why I was yelling.

~

Timisoara, Romania, 2012

My plan is to catch a 5am train but it's a trek to the station and I'm not totally sure of the route. A man with a full 70's handle bar moustache offers a lift and I take it. After a distance we pull up to a set of traffic lights. The hour is early and the roads are bare but a white van with three men in the front pulls up next to us. The men stare directly into the passenger seats of our vehicle.

I suddenly realise I have no idea where I am, whether this is the route to the station, or the name of the man whose car I am in. I also realise I've not made anyone aware of the decision to accept a lift.

The lights change and I'm delivered to the station unscathed. Moustache was just a nice guy offering a favour to a stranger so I live to fumble through another day.

~

Zagreb, Croatia, 2012

The group is planning a trip to Plitvice Lakes tomorrow and the photos are gorgeous. The only problem is that I feel my chest tightening every time I think of going near water.
What if I fall in?
What if I have to board lots of boats?
What if I have a panic attack?
After hours of inner turmoil, I conclude the risk of ruining the trip through fear or crying is too great.
"I'm not coming" I announce, "It's too expensive".

~

Ljubljana, Slovenia, 2012

I arrive alone, enjoying heat from the sun
                But leave in a group, three girls having fun

We see dragons, the river, shoes hanging too
                Then go up to the castle, admire the view

The most picturesque city I've seen, bar none
                And this is the place that I turn twenty one

~

Gdansk, Poland, 2013

I finish reading a book in my comfortable, almost empty, twelve bed dorm and decide to treat myself to an evening meal. It's a short walk to the docks and I feel a great sense of peace in enjoying my own company. I choose a restaurant and am given a window seat overlooking the water while a friendly waiter takes my order and lights a candle. When the main arrives it tastes delicious and as I enjoy the quiet sounds of the evening, snow begins to fall, turning the window into a living postcard.

A perfect moment.

~

Marrakech, Morocco, 2013

Something's wrong.
My body is screaming to get off the coach and run to a safe

place. I pray we miss the flight to Morocco. Someone seems to be listening as we are repeatedly delayed but get to the airport with minutes to spare before gate closing time. Damn. If we'd arrived ten minutes later, we'd be arranging transport home now.

Landed. It's already too hot and humid.
"Like trying to breathe through soup" says Rebecca. The hostel lacks air conditioning and my accommodation is a mattress. Four inches from the floor I lay down with an all-consuming tension headache and try to block out sunlight. There is no escape. My usual tactic of going outside for calm and quiet is stolen by both the blazing heat and the locals who want spare change or for me to make a purchase. I silently cry out to go home but have neither the energy nor cognitive functioning to do anything about it.

Twenty four hours in, my boyfriend texts details of a flight home with my name on it.
After forty eight hours Ellen has printed the boarding pass at an internet cafe and I am on a return flight.

Should you ask me whether I've been to Morocco, my answer will be: No.

Magic Hood

~

I'm anxious, but no worry; I've got my magic hood
     Always helps to shield me,
              when I'm not feeling good

Walk along the roadside, cars and people stare
     But as I am invisible,
              I don't have to care

Strangers stroll towards me, I focus on my feet
     As they cannot see me,
              there's no one here to greet

Arriving at the local shop, frightened and alone
     "Hey, no hoods" security shouts
              So, I run back home

Unstable Relationships
An unrelenting addiction

~

I have had more love interests than I care to admit to and seem to attract a certain type of person. Either I'm a magnet for the dangerous and damaged or I don't relate to stable, wholesome people. Whichever the case I find myself surrounded by broken souls; it probably just makes me feel more 'normal'.

~

She always ended up with me on a night out, probably because she knew she could. I was infatuated, would have gone along with anything, and she knew it. It was never 'official' so I said nothing when she dated other people; always men. But even if her game involved sharing, I'd choose it every time over not having her at all.

~

I passed his place each day on the walk home from work and knew his parked car meant he was inside. I couldn't help but look, something compelled me.
When his drive was empty, my heart would plummet. Where was he? What was he doing? Who was he with?
But the sight of the old Ford meant a later trip to the shops in a desperate attempt to bump into him accidentally-on-purpose.

On the rare occasion I saw him in his lounge I imagined he would have spotted me strolling by. This would be followed by an evening of staring intently at my mobile waiting for his name to flash up whilst experiencing disappointment each time I received a message from someone else.

~

He was quite wonderful but moved away to university so we barely saw each other; travel is expensive for penniless students.
When I ended things he told me I had broken his heart and destroyed his soul.
That sentence will haunt me until I die.

~

Every date was like the first date, and not in a good way. Physical and emotional progression was initially slow, then just stopped. Her issues wouldn't let her lower the wall she had built but each time I tried ending it she assured me she wanted us to continue dating. She would say she had feelings for me one day then treated me like a stranger the next, ending conversations with "Thank you for calling"
I have yet to make sense of that...

~

We were 'just friends'.
He refused to sleep with me but was happy to kiss, cuddle and share a bed. He couldn't sleep without a 'nighty night chat' which often meant him driving to mine at 10pm so we could sit and talk in his car.
I suspected he was in love with a friend of his.

He suspected I was in love with a friend of mine.
We continued our charade until he left the country.

~

He asked me to marry him on our third date.
Eight years later he tracked me down on social media to say
he meant it and stood by his proposal...

Guilt

~

For coming home late, or not at all
For every snide comment, that made you feel small
For trying to make you drink alcohol
And stealing Babychams from the garage

I Am So Sorry

For letting friends sleep on the living room floor
For the ridiculous scene I made while in Wroclaw
For the time I dislocated your jaw
And inviting my boyfriend to Cleethorpes

I Am So Sorry

For the fight that got out of hand in the snow
For crying into a jacket potato
For irrational texts, not letting things go
And the time you found my genital warts cream

I Am So Sorry

For parties I threw when you were away
For not visiting on your last birthday
For choosing to leave, when I knew I should stay
And frightening you with my bad choices

I Am So Sorry

For saying I'd come, then not turning up
For kicking you off the trip round Europe
For losing my patience, storming off in Pembroke
        And spilling tea at the funeral

I Am So Sorry

For hanging out with your friends and embarrassing you
For being distracted, just saying "you too"
For not taking time out to support you
        And letting my mood swings give you whiplash

I Will Always Be Sorry

PART TWO:
PROPER MENTAL

~

Not right in the head

~

Sometimes I say, think or do things I don't quite understand. Usually this happens while experiencing severe symptoms of anxiety or overconfidence. I become over-sensitive, over-feeling, and am caught in thought patterns that wouldn't make sense to me were I in my right mind.
At the time my actions make perfect sense and I don't understand the reactions of others. It's only later when on a saner level of thinking that I begin to question myself.

Occasionally I bump into people who chat about things I've done or events we've been at together and I don't even have facial recognition. I didn't know I'd met them, yet they can recall conversations we've had in great detail.

Speed is another issue. I regularly find the world is going too fast and I can't keep up. Other times I find myself on fast forward with the world trying to slow me down.

These experiences are what scare me most about mental illness: the idea that I can go onto another level of thinking which doesn't match my usual wants and principles; and the knowledge that I can experience emotions so extreme that I act on them in a way I wouldn't normally. It frightens me. As does the apparent forgetfulness and fuzzy half memories I have from these times.

There are people out there who have had interactions with me that I don't know about...

Away with the Fairies

~

In my garden the sunlight is magic. The sky is its brightest blue while the grass and trees are the most perfect green ever seen.

A smile lives on my face as I am full of happy. Physically, my feet touch the ground but spiritually, my life force is connected to the Earth. I feel the earth, the plants, the animals: intentionally connected in harmony. My skin radiates this secret, yet obvious knowledge.

The universe delivered me here for a reason. It is my destiny to awaken our species and help them see our spiritual truth. Every breath I inhale is opportunity. Each exhale stretches my bodily aura. Should you enter my bubble you will feel it; the heartbeat of our planet and the way we are each a stitch in the magnificent tapestry of life and the universe.

Oh, no...
It must be bad if you're here...

~

When I'm scared a six year old takes over my brain.
When I'm angry a fourteen year old gobshite pops out. I've tried explaining this before and it never makes much sense. I don't suffer psychosis nor do I have multiple personalities.

It started when a counsellor tried giving my fourteen year old self a safe space to express her feelings.
Fourteen was my age when I lost my dad, got in with the wrong crowd, and discovered alcohol. I had an all-consuming amount of anger hiding overwhelming grief and sadness.
As far as I can fathom, around the time I was giving young Chelsea a healing platform I also began to recognise and departmentalise my emotions (a subconscious coping strategy?).

So on the (now) rare occasion I am suddenly consumed by anger my thought pattern splits in two:
"I can't f***ing believe he's just said that! What an absolute b******! I'll kill him" teen Chel says
 "Calm down, kidda. Take a deep breath. It'll pass", I reply
"Who does he think he is!?"
"Ay, that's enough now" I say firmly, folding my arms and giving myself a stern look.

SImilarly when I become overwhelmed with anxiety, a small

36

child in my head starts crying:

"Shhhhh, it's alright sweetheart, what's the matter?"

"I'm frightened" she whimpers

"It's okay darling, we'll be home soon"

In my mind's eye, I put an arm around her and stroke her hair. In reality I'm clutching my hands to my chest and hiding my face while strangers assume I've lost my carer and offer me a lollipop.

Meat Guilt

~

During a sensitive period of my life, I looked at meat and saw only corpses. I realised, what is presented to me as food, is actually the murdered bodies of animals. Milk and dairy are the products of raped, pregnant cows and eggs are stolen from hens who may have spent their existence caged.

This shift in thinking is difficult to undo. How can I justify eating a creature who posed me no harm when I could eat an alternative meal not made through suffering? To put it simply: I can't cope with the guilt that comes from eating meat. Sometimes just the smell of meat cooking makes me nauseous.

I can't say I never eat meat but if there is a meat free alternative available I choose it, when I cook I use vegetarian and plant based ingredients, and when sitting down to a vegan meal I take pleasure in knowing no animals were harmed in the making of my dinner.

Unfortunately I have now grown suspicious of food in general. Where has it come from? What chemicals was it grown in? Is it covered in pesticides?

If there's a non-organic field next to an organic field, how does the wind know not to blow pesticides across the boundary line?

I've tried growing my own herbs, veg and fruit with limited success but how do I know which seeds are genetically modified? And when I harvest things I hear a tiny scream in my head, as if the leaves I'm collecting are the lettuces limbs being ripped from its body.

Honestly I try not to think about it anymore, or I'd never eat again.

I Told You This Already, You Just Weren't Listening

~

When in a quiet mood I find I have conversations with people, in my head. I'll sit next to someone chatting away then realise I haven't actually opened my mouth.
"How are you?" I ask
"I'm good thanks, how are you?" they reply "Managing mostly. Struggling a bit with [insert worry here] though"

Whilst this plays out in my mind, neither of us have spoken. So I can think I've had more interactions with people than I have in reality and develop friendships without the other parties' knowledge. In my head, I'm telling you about something I've found traumatic, and you're responding in the way I want you (or need you) to, while we're actually just sat watching television.

I became aware of this after hearing my mum say "sometimes Chelsea thinks she's told you something when she hasn't"
I now have no idea who I've said what to and whether my memories of conversations are real or imaginary.

If you start adding anxiety to the mix I've probably gone through a conversation seven times in my head before it happens. So when I leave I don't know what I actually said versus what I intended to say!
No wonder I'm always repeating myself.

Obsession #372

~

Have you ever loved someone with every fibre of your being?
You can't concentrate as you can't stop thinking about them. You can't remember what life was like before you found them. Couldn't possibly ever live without them…

~

Elvis Presley is the ultimate heartthrob. *Can't Help Falling in Love with You* changes the rhythm of my breathing and brings tears to my eyes.
I'm crying because the love is so pure. I don't believe anyone has ever felt this passionate.

I watch *Blue Hawaii* twenty times. *Viva Las Vegas*, *G.I. Blues*, and *Loving You*, are found in HMV and Fopp. More obscure titles are brought on Amazon and I spend mornings waiting for the postman in need of my next fix!
Albums are purchased one at a time in chronological order of release date. Yes, that includes Christmas albums. My bedroom walls are posters of his beautiful face. I find a specialist shop in the city and visit when I have pocket money: an Elvis purse, brooch, tee shirt.
At school I talk about him and hum favourite songs. Classmates nickname me 'Chelvis'.

My IT coursework is a website making project; I make a site

dedicated to the life of The King. It's easy because I already know his entire life history.

I go to bed and plan the life we will have together from the day we first meet in 1959.

I can't wait until they invent time travel!

~

I LOVE Michael Lee Aday; also known as Meat Loaf. Steinman and Meat are an artistic match made in heaven and the way Meat performs, feels the lyrics and acts out each character is nothing short of incredible. Such passion! Such beauty!

Mum introduced me to the *Bat Out of Hell* album as a child and I've loved it ever since. Other artists come and go, but still I return to Meat Loaf. Michael. Marvin. Because it's true love: it lasts a lifetime!
I never met him. Last time he was touring I waited around, hoping. Knowing he was in close proximity, the same city, but not knowing how to find him. He's back in Vegas now. Maybe he's settling in Vegas? I should go there and seek him out!

I bumped into my friend Matthew earlier. He's started tattooing. Maybe I should visit. Apparently he's practiced on pigskins...
I want 'Meat Loaf'...
In his signature font...
Within a bat...
Inside a heart of my torn flesh...

There's a moral to this one:
Do NOT get tattooed in random bedrooms. No one enjoys an infected swelling and pus blisters are only good for making you want to vomit.

~

Cocktails, shots and alcopops. Ellen and I are heading towards a professional level of drinking when she says
"We should go on a eurotrip!"

And so it begins. I am consumed by possibility. The places we could go! The things we could see!
I read, research, plan a daily route, hostel, activities, food budget, spending money. I have country maps, city maps, train maps. Until I know European geography better than my own county.
I am filled with excitement and it spills out of me! Soon others want to join. Our first stop, Amsterdam, becomes a girl's trip. A friend fancies Italy so I arrange where she can meet us for a week then depart as we continue on to Switzerland. There are so many places and I must see them all!

The result: sixteen countries and twenty eight cities over two summers involving nine people.

~

The Rocky Horror Picture Show.

How Richard O'Brien's brain came up with this masterpiece I will never know! The songs are so catchy, the subject matter so daring, and to have been produced in the 70's;

43

clearly ahead of its time. Every character so unique, the almost ridiculousness of parts giving comedic value, and who doesn't know the *Time Warp*!

I watch the movie again and again. I show anyone who will humour me and try to help them see the beautiful complexity of the themes. I see the stage production; twice. Attend a Halloween cinema showing. Wear the tee shirt-...

Ten years later I have Dr Frank-n-Furter's 'Boss' tattoo on my right arm and am regularly stopped by strangers who want to chat about Bruce Springsteen.

~

372 may be an exaggeration but you see what I'm getting at.

Other passing fixations I would have gladly dedicated my life to, include: Johnny Depp; vintage and antique timepieces; finding a way to emigrate to Canada (a place I have never even visited); comedians Paul Whitehouse and Greg Davies; how to reduce the damage done by the Chernobyl disaster; and of course, alpacas.

Cats, Everywhere

~

Wherever I go, I see cats.
Not actual living, breathing cats, like some sort of animal stalker. But an imaginary cat lurks just beyond my line of sight and I regularly spot her out the corner of my eye.

My understanding of how the brain works is that it doesn't interpret every detail your eyes focus on but grabs a bunch of pixels then fills in the blanks with what it expects to see.
Apparently the thing I most expect to see is a cat approaching.

At home I sense and see in the background of sight, my ginger rat-catcher Nixon appearing through a doorway and strolling out into the garden. But when I stop concentrating on what I'm doing and turn around, Nixon remains asleep behind me.
At work, he trots nonchalantly into a room. Then I realise he can't possibly have travelled several miles and stealthily entered a building without anyone noticing, and it would be ridiculous for that building to then coincidentally turn out to be my workplace. So I do a double take to find nothing sat where I'd have sworn Nixon was a second before.
During my pre-cat life, a slender black feline would wander into my flat. Upon a thorough search no trace of any animal or open windows would be found.

Either this is my experience of deja-vu or I have a short haired domestic with knowing eyes as a spirit animal.

Oops!
Almost gave the game away...

~

After minor surgery I woke in recovery coming around from anaesthetic.

Going under had been odd: I counted down from ten and was still awake; the anaesthetist then grabbed my arm and pushed along my vein until I passed out. Confused and dazed I noticed beds beside me and responded with fright to unknown surroundings.

A woman hovered over me.

"Are you married?" I ask her

"Yes" she replies, and I burst into tears.

I spent most of the day under observation due to concerns I was emotional...

I'm always emotional.

PART THREE:
RANTING AND RAVING

~

That's it! I've had enough now...

~

Mental health seems to be more talked about now than it has been in the past. Even in the years since I reached adulthood I've found more mental health based books hitting the mainstream, more mindfulness magazines in supermarket aisles, and more talk of health and wellbeing in the workplace.

Despite this there are still many people out there that don't understand how mental illness can affect every part of your life. Every friendship group, classroom, and department, has its own mental health denier and person who thinks symptoms are exaggerated, even fabricated.

There is also an institutional lack of support for people who need it. In my experience of depression on the NHS I found that, when at my lowest point and considering how to end my life, I was given medication which takes a minimum of four weeks to begin working and put on a six month waiting list for therapy. The GP couldn't even refer me for therapy, I had to self-refer.

With friends or in the workplace mental health is still a taboo subject which people skirt around if they can. If you break your leg you might receive a Get Well Soon card but don't expect one when you're off with anxiety or if you get sectioned!

I often find mental health to be the elephant in the room. It's such a huge part of my existence and I'm constantly self-managing symptoms, so it crops up when people try getting to know you. Eventually I have to make the conscious decision of whether to 'come out' as mentally ill or avoid answering questions and give vague answers, which keeps people at a distance and isn't really my style.

So here I am, joining the ever growing number of people affected by mental health who are opening up dialogues (and ranting and raving) in the hopes of getting people thinking and bringing about some positive change.

Flavour of the Month

~

The winner of my worst-thing-to-say-to-someone-who's-struggling-with-their-mental-health award goes to a General Practitioner at my local doctors' surgery.

After thirteen years of symptoms and denial. After several mixed and missed diagnoses. I attended a doctor's appointment to discuss a psychiatric referral, as suggested by my usual GP. With the help of close family I researched bipolar disorder and went to the appointment with a list of symptoms and a sense of hope.
I did not receive a referral. Instead, I met a man who openly laughed at some of my symptoms and disregarded my concerns. Bipolar disorder was the 'flavour of the month' he said; lots of people are claiming they have it!

Firstly, it's not okay to brush off distressing symptoms. Secondly, this attitude is poor, especially from a physician. And thirdly, anyone who claims to have a psychiatric disorder probably needs a psychiatric assessment.

If you're wondering what other little gems made my top ten, here they are:

"You have nothing to be sad about!"
...Other than crippling symptoms of depression

"What, you're *still* ill?"

Yes, I *still* have an incurable illness.

"It's because you're a woman"
I have yet to decide whether this is more offensive to women, or men with mental health issues. Perhaps I actually appear more rational to some by belonging to a gender they consider irrational! Either way, there are no points here for gender equality.

"Depression is just an excuse to not work"
Being well and at work is preferable to being stuck in bed screaming. Trust me.

"Time heals all wounds"
...Does it also heal chemical imbalances?

"It's all in your head"
...Well, duh! Where else would it be?

"Self-harm is just attention seeking"
It's not. But if you genuinely believe that, be grateful you're not so desperate for attention you'd be willing to hurt yourself.

"You need a change of perspective"
Yes! That would be great!
...How do I do that, exactly?

"I don't believe in personality disorders"
...Thanks for the support!

Daylight Saving Time

~

October is the worst month. The clocks go back. Or forward? I've yet to get the hang of it. March is easier to cope with but I could still do without it.

Months are spent getting into a daily routine of sleeping, waking up, eating regularly, perhaps going to work at the same time each day. Then BAM! The whole country decides to change what time it is and you're back to square one: waking up at 6am, thinking its 7 but apparently its 5; turning up to appointments on the wrong day, or at the wrong time; arriving at the end of a university lecture thinking it's the start time.

I dread the tenth month on the calendar whose only function is to engulf me in a cloud of confusion.
Is it just me?

The Needless Pressure of the Mobile Phone

~

Being contactable twenty four hours of the day is totally unnecessary. Unless you suffer from a major illness or are going on a hike where you may get lost, be mauled by a bear and require emergency services, the chances of actually needing the phone in your pocket are pretty slim.
Mobile phones are now portable entertainment systems. They help you avoid greeting the till operator at the supermarket checkout and distract you on your commute so you miss your stop on the bus.

For me a ringing phone can be a huge cause of anxiety. I work a shift pattern and love working evenings and weekends for one reason; I'm not constantly on edge staring at the office phone. Whether at work or home, not having a phone gives me one less thing to worry about. The noise alone makes me jump out of my skin, I don't know who I'm going to be speaking to, and I can't use body language to help me communicate.

I also resent the idea that people expect to contact me at any time. If I'm not at work, there's no reason for my line manager to be calling me. If I haven't immediately texted back I'm not ignoring you, I've probably just gone for a walk and left my phone in a drawer where it can't panic me. Don't make me feel guilty for not using a phone in the instant way you want me to.

If phones put you on edge or the thought of going out without one is terrifying then you should probably give it a try. You'll soon discover you continue living and breathing and that your phone isn't an extension of your body.
If nothing else, you'll get a break from scammers and PPI.

Me, On Screen Again

~

Watching television recently I found myself amused by a character who reminded me of me, particularly during periods of illness. Needless to say by the end of the episode her bipolar status had been revealed.

Whilst I suspected this within two minutes of the programme starting it made me wonder why her behaviours seemed so familiar. Of course people with similar conditions could have similar symptoms but the same responses, thoughts and behaviours? Do I not have my own personality? Am I just a stereotype of 'manic depressive' with no further depth or substance? Are my actions my own or the responses of a chemical imbalance?

In short: Do I have ANY control of myself?

If my feelings are manufactured by a wonky brain and my thoughts are common to those with a 'bipolar' label then, who am I?

Where does the illness end and I begin?

If my brain is reactive does that mean everything I do is predetermined?

Are the only actions that are 'mine' those I make consciously and with consideration?

Who makes decisions when I'm not feeling myself?

Who makes those decisions I don't understand later on?

This is why I try not to think too much. It's exhausting.

The Disability Box

~

I hate this box. Do I consider myself disabled? When applying for a job there are three options: Yes, No, Prefer not to disclose.

Yes: Rule yourself out as a potential candidate. You can scream 'equality and diversity' as much as you like but if it puts someone off employing you they'll find a way around it.

No: Spend your time at work hiding your illness and ensure the company isn't liable should you need any reasonable adjustments as you did not initially make the disclosure.

Prefer not to disclose: Implies a yes and refuses to answer a question, which could be interpreted as suspicious, non-cooperative or as showing a lack of commitment to the organisation by not answering questions before you've even started.

Usually this question is amongst a number of personal questions which will 'not be considered' in the recruitment process. It's just a casual look into the demographics the company's jobs are attracting; a positive step to ensure groups of people aren't inadvertently excluded from wanting to work for them.

Yet I have genuinely sat in a job interview where one panel member turned to another and asked:

"Did the equality and diversity sheet check out?"
To which his colleague replied "yes"

I also take issue with the word 'consider'. To me, this includes an accusation that I don't have a disability and am either delusional, or fabricating an illness.

Yes?
No?
Prefer not to disclose?
Whatever answer will get me the job!

No, I Still Can't Drive

~

This is such a sore subject for me and I've been haunted by it for at least a decade.

Education has always come easy to me; I've sat exams drunk and still passed. In fact I've experienced an examination from a viewpoint I can only describe as looking down, floating above my body and still managed a B grade. But for me, being in control of a crate of metal on wheels just doesn't work.

There's so much going on when you're driving. Just being aware of your surroundings is overwhelming: cars, pedestrians, traffic lights, multiple lanes, zebra crossings, road signs, upcoming junctions, cyclists, and parked vehicles to overtake. Not to mention whatever's behind you. Everywhere you look there's something ready and waiting to pounce. I failed my hazard perception test and I'm convinced it's because I saw more potential death traps than the DVLA.

Then there's the actual driving part: balancing a clutch at biting point; whilst beginning to accelerate; whilst releasing the hand break; whilst manoeuvring the steering wheel; and still keeping that awareness of all 360 degrees, including some mysterious 'blind spot' that eludes me. How people do this every day without their brains exploding I'll never understand. Just the thought of it gives me a headache.

My usual 'have a go and see what happens' approach to life, even during a hypomanic episode, doesn't extend to my co-ordination.

Strangely, I am a decent driver. Despite feeling two moves away from a crash whenever I'm behind a wheel I seem to pull it off smoothly for the most part. At least two of my three former driving instructors were confident in my ability. I had a Renault Megane for a while too, L plates included. I've driven in snowstorms, around city centres and up hills I wouldn't attempt on foot. Driving takes a huge amount of concentration and I'm mentally exhausted for a while afterwards, but it's doable.

The problem comes when you add the pressure of a driving test to the mix; turning the nervous driving panic into a category A melt down. It doesn't matter how long I've been driving competently for, sit an examiner next to me and I'll make silly mistakes, mess up manoeuvres and miss obvious road signs.
My first test resulted in zero minors but two majors, which is an impressive achievement. The last test involved the examiner panicking, leading me to hyperventilate, pull over and refuse to continue.

Over five years later I gave driving another try but found I had the same category A response to a mock test. That instructor suggested I see a head doctor, as I clearly had a psychological trigger preventing me driving. That was after weeks of him telling me how beautiful I was as he thought I had a confidence issue...

But beyond my broken psyche and odd instructors the societal attitude towards driving makes my inability even worse. My limited employability (who really wants to hire a head case, and what job could I do that won't end in me cracking under pressure?) is further limited by my reliance on public transport. People also assume you can drive and expect it. I've been encouraged and given a nudge towards promotions then had them retracted because someone might want me to work from a different site occasionally. If I've managed to rely on public transport and arranging lifts this far in my life, I think I'd sometimes manage to get to a different building for the ten grand pay rise you were just thrusting towards me!

Why don't I drive, you ask?
I don't like it;
It's difficult, exhausting and expensive;
My feet belong firmly on the ground;
I prefer to be chauffeured.

Choose any of the above; I'm tired of making excuses.

Positive Fucking Thinking

~

I'll try to spell this out because some people can't comprehend this.

If you have a chemical imbalance like depression, an inability to think positively is an actual symptom. You can't find a way to think positive; that's part of the illness.

Telling someone to think positive is telling them they have a choice and are choosing to think negatively. This denies any clinical illness and plays the blame game. You are disregarding feelings, telling people they are choosing to have an illness and putting someone down, who is already feeling down.

Positive thinking has its place as a coping strategy but it is far from a cure.

PART FOUR:
ACCEPTANCE

~

I'm not the average person. I have a mental illness.
It's not something that can be fixed. And that's okay.

~

After realising I had an illness that needed to be addressed I did what most people probably do: I tried to fix it.

I tried medications, I followed doctor's orders and I self-referred to a local mental health charity who gave me strategies to try out at home.

Six months later my mood lifted and I made the following conclusion: I had cured myself!

How silly of me to never have considered my mental health before, I just needed a bit of mindfulness! So I did what any rational person would do: I stopped taking my medication.

As you may have worked out from the title of this book alone, that was not the end of my mental health journey.

I managed roughly a year un-medicated, mostly bouncing

between numbness and anxiety. I kept a job by going to work, then going home, then going back to work, and doing absolutely nothing else. I pushed away the people who were aware of my previous 'little bout of depression' and resented anyone who showed concern for my mood, isolated lifestyle or odd behaviours.

This continued until I received some bad news which triggered a complete mental break and instead of scraping by on the borderline of normalcy, I fell head first into the depressive pit. I found myself back at square one, possibly even square minus one as I had also stopped eating. In a matter of weeks I had gone from an already thin size 10 to a frighteningly skeletal size 6.

This second bout of severe depression forced me to realise that I had not 'cured myself'; I'd just accepted the existence of mental health and managed my symptoms well for a time.

I recognised times in my life where I had experienced mild-moderate depression or anxiety. I realised specific behaviours which were symptoms rather than choices. Then eventually, after seeing various medical professionals and actually listening to my friends and family, I accepted that my illness was not temporary.

This was not going away, it wasn't going to be fixed and I needed to learn to live with it.

Busy Bee VS Hibernating Bear

~

I have friends who never seem to stop. They barely sit down between family commitments, day trips, work, and going on holidays. When I ask if they're free they're booked up until Christmas, despite it being spring;
"I'm with family Saturday, then sky diving Sunday, then I'm working away for a week, then I'm popping to Albania to check out South-East Europe..."

Firstly, these types clearly earn more than my minimum wage stint. But when do they stop? When do they sleep? Does it catch up to them? Are they really that full of energy? Is it all just distraction techniques?

I am a hibernating bear. When those dark nights come in November my body yearns for its cave. I slow down physically and mentally. Just looking at a full calendar makes me tired and sometimes anxious.
At this point, I start my Christmas shopping in October, so it doesn't creep up and smother me when December comes. I am trudging through life, slowly and heavily, and I'm mostly okay with that. When I'm energetic and excitable I'll make plans, but when I'm not you won't find me running to keep up. I'll have checked out of the race and you'll notice me quietly spectating. I'll even cheer you on... if I have the energy!

I Refuse to Feel Ashamed

~

At this point in my life, I have surpassed shame. Don't worry; I gave him a little wave as I left.

I refuse to feel ashamed when I'm too ill to work or find something unusually difficult. I may be an over emotional, reactive person but my feelings are still valid. If you disagree, I'm afraid my cup of care is empty.

Pretending is exhausting. Pretending to be happy, pretending to be normal. Keeping quiet because what I say may make someone laugh, or frown, get angry, perhaps have me sectioned. So I will now be open and honest. It's not that I'm rude, or cruel, I'm just not scared anymore. For example, two years ago I attended a wedding and the person next to me asked what I do for a living.

"I don't work because I'm mental", I responded. Evidently I'd sat with the right person as she said "Me too".

This meeting led me to a local support group of which I'm still a member.

Part of the reason I don't mind if people know I have mental health issues (or think I'm odd), is that I have a strong support network of close friends and family who love me regardless. I also won't benefit by having people in my life who think I shouldn't discuss my problems or who find me embarrassing.

Another part of my blunt, lack of shame is self-preservation.

If I make a friend but have to cancel an outing hopefully they will understand and know it's just me having brain-ache, instead of being offended. If a colleague is aware that I'm struggling they might be willing to help me if I ask for support instead of thinking I'm just lazy.

My mental health is inconvenient, tiring and constantly getting in the way. I spend a lot of time self-managing and it's taken a long time for me to accept myself. So I will no longer be ashamed of my brain, I will not be embarrassed of having an illness and I will not live in fear of being judged.

Accepting My Normal

~

It happened again.

I thought I was past this. I thought I had learned to manage my illness and cope with symptoms. But here I am again, in a GP's surgery, asking a doctor for a sick note.

I've spent years in therapy, I constantly police myself, checking in on my moods and behaviours, acknowledging what my body is craving, using relaxation techniques to keep myself calm.
Yet, here I am; overwhelmed, having left work in tears. I'm anxiously sat in a familiar waiting room, hoping for a sympathetic doctor, knowing there's no quick fix and they may try to avoid signing me off work; especially if it's a GP who doesn't take mental health seriously.

I am so disappointed. I've gone months without having time off or having to consider how many hours I'm able to work each week. I've followed my management plan and used my toolbox of tricks. Nevertheless, the shadow has descended. The bear has growled and I'm back in his clutches.

Why can't I be normal? Why can't I just have a job and feel okay? I don't even need to feel good, just okay.

I suppose this is normal: this is my normal.
Up, down, happy, sad; experiencing a world of emotion

whilst trying to function.

I am an outlier on the emotional graph of society and need to spend a lot of my time focusing on self-care.

Maybe this is something else to accept: I'm not always able to work, it's okay to call in sick when I'm ill and reduced working hours might be best from time to time.

I wish it would go away instead though...

The Issue of Employment

~

Why are we so defined by what we do for a living? Is it a status issue for people who live to work or do we judge a person's character based on how they earn money?

When my mental health is poor, I'm unable to work. I'm unable to do most things. Even eat, sleep or speak. It's not that I don't want to, more like my body doesn't respond. It's such a useless feeling. I imagine it to be like stage fright; wanting to get up and perform but you find you can't sing/dance/move.

I'm just trying to get up and make a sandwich.

~

Before I accepted alcohol was an enemy, I used it in the evenings. I mostly drank vodka and was sick in the work toilets in a morning. I kept packets of 'emergency' ibuprofen in my desk and replaced them weekly.

~

A short time in an office with no windows had me walking out with severe depression. I'd been reaching the toilets when I couldn't contain a little cry but once my clouded mind realised the only way out was death, I got up and went home. It's only down to good people, and the fact I was excellent in that role (if I do say so myself!) that I kept that job for another year.

~

A lost appetite resulted in walking out of an admin job, never to return. I'd barely eaten for weeks and my clothes didn't fit anymore. But when the feeling of collapse came over me, I ran. There was no way I would succumb to exhaustion at work, how would I explain it? What if they phoned an ambulance? So I got out the building as fast as I could and never went back.

~

When I consider my illness, I'm oddly impressed with what I've achieved at work. I have often managed being good at a job, met deadlines and been told I'm an asset to the team, whilst scarily undernourished, battling suicidal ideations, or becoming reliant on alcohol to get me through the days. Despite my mistakes, I always try my hardest to earn a living and be good at the things I do.

I don't think you can ask much more of me than that.

Dream Closure

~

As a teenager and young adult I had a complicated relationship with sex. I went through a repetitive cycle of emotion: excitement, lust, infatuation, rejection, disappointment, hatred, and repeat.

In 2019 I married my best friend and soul mate, we had a gorgeous wedding surrounded by our nearest and dearest and I went from being a 'Miss' to a 'Mrs'.

For weeks before and after the big day a dream series of past relationships interrupted my sleep. It was as though my brain said, "That's enough now, time for some closure". While I slept, a long forgotten flame was plucked from Pandora's Box and emotionally explored. These vivid dreams would stay with me the following day as I remembered past events, rationalised experiences and closed the book on an ex love interest with acceptance, often fondness, and occasionally resignation.
Once a little time had passed and Exhibit A had faded back into (a now less painful) memory, I would find myself in another dream, with another subject of my past.

While it could be confusing, painful, or cringe worthy, it also felt like healing. To realise each person had moved on, just as I had, accepting I cannot change past feelings or behaviour, forgiving them (occasionally) and myself (often), then letting go.

Warning:
Human Parasite Present

~

I am a leech. Where I go I cling onto people, sucking up their emotional reserves and using them as my own.

When out with family I link arms or hold hands and force them to lead while I emotionally lean on them. If out in a group I choose a friend to cling to like an infant, hiding behind them, making me their responsibility.

Wherever I work I have a work mum or work husband; a go-to person I can depend on in times of stress. If I can make it look like teamwork it actually wins me brownie points with supervisors!

I always rent, so when there's a maintenance issue I can contact the landlord and pass him the responsibility of fixing it. I get friendly with neighbours so when I can't handle my mind chatter I have a go-to person in the immediate vicinity and disguise it as a coffee and a catch up.

The more people care, the more reliable they become, the more likely they are to drop everything and offer support when I'm mid-meltdown.

I pretend to be independent and capable but in truth, I can't cope with anything. I need constant support and set people up around me as safety nets. When I think a friend is getting

tired of dealing with me, I move on to the next one for a while.
Consider this my warning label.

PART FIVE: TIPS AND TRICKS

~

I don't know what I need,
but I definitely need something...

~

I can't help you swim; I'm too busy trying to keep myself afloat. In some ways I don't think anyone can tell you how to live or what to do to feel better when you're struggling. Only you can figure out what works to ease your symptoms or soothe your soul. Only you can acknowledge things that help then choose to do more of them.

What I can do is tell you things that have helped me. If any of my ramblings have resonated with you, or reminded you of someone you know, then we may have similar symptoms or experiences. So, the things that make me feel better may make you feel better too.
There's no harm in trying.

Choosing to Pay Attention:
Monks, monasteries and meditation

~

Of the things I've tried to aid self-soothing, meditation is the best. It doesn't work every time and occasionally frightened me when I first got into it (something about being alone with my thoughts was quite terrifying). But if you want to have a go at something new I'd recommend meditation to anyone.

~

I enter an exquisite Victorian building which began as two large houses. Although doors have been added to allow access to both former residences the building still boasts many of its original features.

After being greeted by a friendly man who requests my name, I am shown a waiting area where I am asked to remove my shoes before entering the 'Meditation room'. Why the room is so named becomes immediately clear as I step barefoot onto the plush beige carpet. Then, creeping as quietly as I am able, I choose an empty chair on the back row. A dozen chairs are set out, along with meditation cushions and blankets. Facing the chairs a wall-length glass cabinet contains Buddha statues of varying size and colour. The room feels soft and silent which I imagine to have been the designer's intention. After a few short minutes my body relaxes and I sink into both chair and carpet while a monk in orange robes places herself in full-lotus on a raised platform and we begin.

Focusing on the breath is more difficult than it sounds, so while my mind repeatedly tries asking "Where are we going after this?" and "What's for dinner?" I try counting each breath I take, in and out. This seems to work, anchoring me to my chest as my breathing deepens and my muscles stop fighting the need to be constantly rigid. I enjoy a few peaceful moments then, when I begin to hope my stomach doesn't rumble loudly and echo around the room, I bring myself back to the breath and count again from one.

The next meditation involves turning our bodies into light. My body is the opposite of light; heavy, solid and far from having the transparent skin the monk is describing. After several attempts to follow the process and failing spectacularly I open my eyes, taking in the room's peace and enjoy birds twittering in the nearby garden.

When I leave, I feel calm and collected. All nerves have departed and my over-anxious body finally gets the respite it deserves.

~

Warrior pose: A favourite in Qi Gong. The slow easy movements focus on connecting to the Earth's energies rather than increasing strength, as you may expect from Pilates or Yoga. It perfectly suits my fitness level: Zero.
I am at a monastery near Huddersfield where I have purposefully subjected myself to a weekend of complete silence. I paid several hundred pounds and travelled miles from home in order to not communicate with another living soul, for two days. Food is provided as a silent buffet and an

area is set out for us to ignore each other in. Activities are listed on the library door which includes meditation, Qi Gong and more meditation.

The weekend is magnificent. I sit, sleep and breathe. I get up at 6am to read, draw and write poetry. I attend most meditation sessions, experiencing mixed success, and practice Qi Gong. I eat, focusing mostly on the taste and texture of each food item. I enjoy the lack of expectation to make conversation and I discover black coffee, as I can't ask anyone where the milk is.

~

A meditative walk focuses entirely on the senses, reminding you how to see. We are being led so I need not fear my awful sense of direction and instead focus on what's in front of me: trees and a path. But not just trees as I have seen them a thousand times before. It's the rough texture of a deep brown bark with grooves where his old skin has cracked, dead leaves delicately breaking under foot, the smell of the cold and the rush of air entering my nostrils.

I hear a rustle from the high reaches as a squirrel leaps from one branch to another, then birds chatting, probably wondering why the humans below are staring at them.
"How many greens can you see?" asks our leader
Suddenly, I realise I am surrounded by an entire spectrum of green! I see different greens for different trees and acknowledge light and shadow enhancing or dulling the natural shades: the same space but in high definition.

There's Nothing Wrong with a Comfort Blanket

~

We're happy with comfort blankets as a soothing technique for children so why not adults? Does it really matter if I keep a fur rug on my office chair to stroke when I'm feeling stressed?

It doesn't even need to be a blanket, you can keep any object around if it makes you feel better. I have a plush Llama named Cusco who was a Christmas gift from a wonderful human and friend. I sleep with him on lonely nights, he chills with me on emotional days and he's my bodyguard when I'm feeling vulnerable. He comes to work with me when I'm not feeling strong and sits inconspicuously around the house when he's not needed.

I'm not suggesting anyone go out and purchase a dummy but the things that brought comfort when you were young may still help now you're grown. Consider it nostalgia!

Be Creative

~

There's a sense of achievement you get when you finish something. Especially if you've done it well or surprised yourself with a little talent. It's a small feeling of pride. An inner well done. Even when the end result is laughable you've achieved something by seeing it through, expressing yourself, perhaps even trying something different.

Drawing, painting and crafts are an excellent choice, there's an obvious achievement when a blank sheet is transformed into picture. When you can't face a blank sheet try collage or mindful colouring. If art isn't your thing, try woodwork, writing, blogging, or baking. It all gives you an end result.

Focusing also takes your mind away from other things. Concentrating on colouring inside the lines, putting pen to paper, or weighing out ingredients, is all time away from niggling worries.

I'm writing this in winter while my GP thinks I am Seasonal Affective; a lovely new addition to my list of disorders. I have been subscribed an hour each day in front of a SAD lamp (although lamp is an understatement, it's about the size of a springer spaniel). But being forced to sit at a desk each day subtly encourages me to do something table based. Today that means writing, yesterday was card-making and tomorrow, who knows, maybe just an hour of doodling. Even if the lamp fails to trigger those sunshine hormones, taking an hour away from my to-do list to achieve something small will lift my mood, even just for a short while.

Choose Your Support Network
Surround yourself with good people

~

I am lucky in having a social network of understanding people I can rely on. My sister is one of these lovelies.

Big sisters are the responsible siblings who look after you, reliably take control and lead when you can only follow. My sister is the perfect big sister: she spends time with me, taking me for walks when I'm depressed; she helped collect my belongings when I lost a flat to my illness; when I stopped eating, she drove to my house to give me a sandwich; and when our mum is at work, she sends the daily text to check in on me and ask how I'm feeling.

One Christmastime, I was off work on sick leave. I could no longer ignore the voice in my head which wanted me to lock myself in my flat and take sleeping pills until my body gave out. The instruction from the GP (ignoring the suggestion "Have you tried swimming?" which just had me wondering how to drown myself) was to stay with family who could care for me and phone emergency services should I attempt suicide. So at the age of twenty three, I found myself back home and sharing a bed with my mother.

On a crisp winter morning, zombied out on mum's sofa, *Stay Another Day* by East 17 began to play on the radio, and my sister did something which turned out to be a profound moment in my life. She sat next to me and said, as if to no one

"He wrote this about his brother's suicide"

Not only did this transform a song I had heard a dozen times every Christmas, it hit me that despite being a burden (and annoying, hard work, miserable, useless etc.), if something happened to me there are people around who might be genuinely upset; an idea which had never occurred to me before.

Although that wasn't the final time I would put a plan together to end my life, it is a memory I pull out as motivation to get help when I am struggling. Should I notice I'm spiralling downhill I put things in place and speak to the right people before I get into that headspace where nothing is rational. Then I won't fall down, far enough to distress those who are most important.

So whenever you can, surround yourself with people who love you, people you can open up to and who might just say something you can cling to when sanity frays at the edges.

Oh, and my wonderful sister who helps look after me, is actually four years younger than I am.

Choose Your Support Network
Weed out bad influences

~

While some friendships, relationships and family members are positive, other relationships are poison.

It may be that your personalities clash or are too similar. A friend may be a bad influence or make you feel down or bad about yourself. Your mission, should you choose to accept it, is to weed out the negative and surround yourself with positivity and lovely people.

This doesn't have to mean cutting people out entirely, although that may be wise in some scenarios. You can spend less time with negative influences, more time with positive ones and arrange to see people on your terms when you feel strong enough to engage with them.

After giving up alcohol I realised some of my friends where just associates with whom I had drinking in common. There were also friends who would encourage me to drink and who I had to have stricter relationships with; I would happily meet for lunch or a coffee, but would refuse any pub meets.

~

A few examples of weed-able characters:

A friend who brings out the worst in you or encourages habits you're trying to break: they're fine when you feel strong but negative when you're delicate and easily led.

Anyone who makes you feel bad about yourself should be avoided like the plague: don't subject yourself to it, they're probably just insecure and trying to take you down with them.

People you 'put up' with; because, what's the point? If you're not a good fit, don't waste precious energy.

Take the common sense approach:
Avoiding smoking? Don't hang around smokers.
Feeling down? Don't spend the day with Eeyore.

~

Weeding is definitely easier said than done. It will be especially hard if you lack confidence, are a people pleaser or struggle with confrontation. But ultimately you should consider what (and who) is best for you. Practise letting people down gently:
"I'd love to, but I really need some time alone at the moment" or;
"I'm having a pub-free February, but I'll meet you for a coffee if you're up for it?"

It's Okay to be Selfish

~

We generally consider selfishness to be a bad character trait: We don't like selfish people. But if you think of it as self-preservation, selfishness can be a great thing. I'm sure there are folk out there who live a selfless life without issue and if we were all capable of that the world would be bliss. But in my experience, selflessness has a limit and you can only give for so long until it becomes detrimental to your wellbeing. So don't feel guilty for putting yourself first, it will help you avoid exhaustion and probably make you happier too. Plus, when you're happy and mentally stable you give out good vibes and find it easier to be helpful and selfless, without feeling stressed or resentful about it!

~

To achieve selfishness I recommend the following:

1 - Realise it's okay to say no.
Even if you're a giving person and love to help others, you can't do everything. There can also be a knock on effect where when you always say yes, those around you expect you to say yes and ask more of you. But 'yes' is optional, other answers are out there if you look for them!
Consider a request before you agree to it. Ask yourself whether you want to do it, if you'll get anything out of it, and if you even can do it or whether it'll cause you distress.
If the answers are no, then say so. 'Yes' doesn't have to be

an automatic response.

2 - Take time out for yourself.
You don't need to constantly be on the go. Taking time out to do nothing or to do something you enjoy is a great way to destress and achieve some calm. If it boosts your mood then others will benefit anyway as your depleted mental-health-bar refills. If there's a specific activity you know helps you feel most like yourself then schedule time in for it, you might feel more relaxed just knowing a time out is on the way.

3 - Remember that you're important too.
I struggle with this. Other people matter and I don't. Other people are important but I'm not. In reality we are all just as important, and unimportant, as each other. So when you get the urge to do something for someone else: Why can't they do it?
Your time and effort is just as important as anyone else's, so choose what you want to do with it.

Consider Your Dreams
They might teach you something

~

I can judge the state of my mental health based on the dream I had last night.

As I understand it the dream part of sleeping is the body trying to repair your mental health, in the same way other parts of sleeping repair the physical body. I like this theory as it fits my experience of dreaming.

When I am in good health I have easy dreams. They may not be happy, perhaps random or surreal, but they are simple meaningless dreams which I have to grasp at to remember the following day. However during times of illness or distress my dreaming experience transforms into vivid, real feeling horror. My dreams are full of colour, heightened emotion, and are usually of either sexually disturbing or horrifically violent content. At their worst I can be ripped from my sleep by the sound of my heart beating, in a state of total anxiety.

So now my dreams are a tool provided by the subconscious. They can benchmark moods and judge when I need to take a time out to care for my mental health.

Get Professional Help

~

Mental health support can be difficult to find. That's coming from someone who actively goes out looking for it.

One to one therapy with a qualified professional is probably the best chance you have at dealing with issues and learning to manage symptoms of an illness. So if you think you need a referral for mental health assistance, ask your GP about local services.

In England this can be a six month waiting list on the NHS. Even then you may not be paired with a practitioner who works well with you, and you'll probably be limited to six sessions; which is just about the amount of time you need to have gotten comfortable enough to go to the appointment without panicking and are beginning to talk freely.

If you're in employment ask the Human Resources department about therapy or counselling, they will have a policy for this. Some companies now outsource to counselling services so your workplace won't necessarily get any information of why you're accessing support.

Other than letting work know you're struggling (if they have a decent employee health plan to start with), or spending months in limbo waiting for an appointment while hoping your symptoms don't worsen in the meantime, you have the option of going private. Be warned: I've spent up to £300 a month on private counselling. So do the math and only arrange sessions for when you can afford them (if you can afford them).

Group therapy and mental health courses may run in your area but in the health sector, location becomes strangely important. I found a course focusing on managing anxiety which sounded promising. Unfortunately I discovered I was out of catchment because I lived two miles too far north to qualify for a place. The centre my 'Community' Mental Health Team falls under has also required me to travel thirteen miles, using multiple methods of transport, to access support and assessments. Of course, the worse your illness is the more you need the support and the harder it is to make a twenty six mile round trip!

Look out for local independent support groups. They may not involve professionals, some are set up by individuals aiming to help other people with a similar illness, but they can give emotional support and point you in the right direction. Independent support groups often specialise in something specific, like bipolar disorder or anxiety. They can be intimate too, with a small number of regular members. So in the initial introduction you may find yourself the stranger in a group who are already comfortable together. I tried a few groups before finding one I slotted into nicely, after eighteen months I'm still the newest member!
One group I considered seemed more church based than I was comfortable with, another focused wholly on anxiety, which is a symptom for me but not my entire illness. My support group is a mixture of illnesses, ages and characters; which suits me fine! I can discuss anything I need to without judgement or fear of upsetting anyone.

An online search for local groups should signpost you to potential support in your area and there may also be listings in your local newspaper and magazines.

Good luck and happy searching!

Stop Playing the Comparison Game

~

Please stop comparing yourself to other people. You are not other people. You are your own unique self. Every person out there is a mixture of abilities, characteristics and preferences. Maybe you can't run a marathon, but have fantastic hair and are a local chess champion. Maybe you can run a marathon, but never got around to learning how to read or tie shoelaces. Honestly, it doesn't matter. We all have things we're good at, bad at, struggle with and fear. Even if someone seems to have it all it doesn't mean that's actually the case. Envy, jealousy, resentment; it's all just negative energy that will make you feel worse about your own situation.

~

A few years ago I began a new job and on starting the role, I found my line manager was younger than me. I was to take orders and suggestions from someone in their early twenties who had never had another job and still lived with her parents.

Unfortunately I was guilty of ageism and felt my superior should have more work and life experience than I had. But mostly I felt cheated (and jealous).

She had walked into a job, liked it, and made an impression. She had a career plan; a genuine 'five year plan'.

I couldn't get past it. I couldn't help but wonder if, had I not been mentally defective, that could have been me. If I'd never had to hit pause and have time out of work, would I be confident enough to go for management roles? If I hadn't impulsively changed jobs, swapping the education sector for the charity sector for the corporate sector, would I have moved up instead of horizontally? If anxiety hadn't overcome me during my driving tests, would a world of employment opportunities have opened up for me?

If I could handle pressure, would I be a high-flier?

~

In truth, mental illness massively impacts my life and without it I'd be a different person. It isn't fair that I was dealt a wonky set of cards but it's the only hand I've got. Comparing my successes (or lack thereof) to other people's helps nothing. Having accepted that, I can genuinely celebrate other people's achievements without a little green man on my shoulder. I can congratulate people on important successes in their lives, regardless how big or small.

I'm a nicer person; to others and to myself.

FINAL WORDS
What now?

~

Recognising you need help is hard and accessing help is even harder.

If you think you have an undiagnosed mental illness please visit your GP, I've also included a list of UK based support groups and charities which you may find useful.

If you read this book out of curiosity, or because you are the friend or relative of a sufferer, then I thank you for taking an interest in mental health and have included a few mental health related titles you may find of interest for further reading.

To any fellow sufferers of mental illness: thank you for reading. I hope my story helped, resonated with you or at least made you laugh once or twice. I hope I did a decent job of showing some of the difficulties of living with a mental illness and, should you try any of my tips and tricks, I hope they make things easier for you, as they have for me.

For every time you've kept on fighting; well done and be proud.

For every hard time to come; be brave and stay strong. Ask for help when you need it and appreciate those who are willing to provide it.

Sending love vibes.

Chelsea x

Mental Health Support (UK)

~

Details accurate at time of publishing
Always call 999 during a crisis

~

Mind

The Mind website contains user friendly reading about different conditions, signs and symptoms to help you understand a diagnosis. They publish real life stories on their blog and phone lines are confidential.
Web: www.mind.org.uk
Tel: 0300 123 3393

Samaritans

The Samaritans phone line is available twenty four hours a day, all year round.
Web: www.samaritans.org
Tel: 116 123

Rethink

The Rethink website lists help groups and services in your local area, just enter your town/city and see what is available close to home.
Web: www.rethink.org

Reading

~

There are an increasing number of mental health related books, websites and magazines being published. Some focus on how to cope with symptoms of mental health, others explore living with such conditions and all are a great step towards accepting mental health in our society.

These are a few items which have genuinely helped me understand my condition and combat various symptoms:

John Parkin, F**k It: The Ultimate Spiritual Way
(Hay House, 2010)

The Diagnostic and Statistical Manual of Mental Disorders, Fifth Edition
(American Psychiatric Association, 2013)

www.Iam1in4.com
(Website)

In the Moment
(Magazine; Immediate Media Co)

Benjamin Hoff, The Tao of Pooh
(Egmont, 2018)

Printed in Poland
by Amazon Fulfillment
Poland Sp. z o.o., Wrocław

57649834R00066